Feeling Angry

by Rosalyn Clark

LERNER PUBLICATIONS ◆ MINNEAPOLIS

Note to Educators:

Throughout this book, you'll find critical thinking questions. These can be used to engage young readers in thinking critically about the topic and in using the text and photos to do so.

Lerner Publications Company
A division of Lerner Publishing Group, Inc.
241 First Avenue North
Minneapolis, MN 55401 USA

For reading levels and more information, look up this title at www.lernerbooks.com.

Library of Congress Cataloging-in-Publication Data

Names: Clark, Rosalyn, 1990–
Title: Feeling angry / Rosalyn Clark.
Description: Minneapolis : Lerner Publications, c2018. | Series: Bumba books. Feelings matter | Audience: Age 4–7. |
    Audience: K to grade 3. | Includes bibliographical references and index.
Identifiers: LCCN 2017002406 (print) | LCCN 2017015560 (ebook) | ISBN 9781512450262 (eb pdf) | ISBN 9781512433708 (lb :
    alk. paper) | ISBN 9781512455465 (pb : alk. paper)
Subjects: LCSH: Anger in children—Juvenile literature. | Anger—Juvenile literature.
Classification: LCC BF723.A4 (ebook) | LCC BF723.A4 C53 2018 (print) | DDC 152.4/7—dc23
LC record available at https://lccn.loc.gov/2017002406

Manufactured in the United States of America
1 – CG – 7/15/17

Expand learning beyond the printed book. Download free, complementary educational resources for this book from our website, www.lerneresource.com.

Table of Contents

Feeling Angry

Anger is a feeling.

What makes you feel angry?

Maybe you broke your

favorite toy.

It was an accident.

But you feel angry.

Maybe your mom asked you

to do a chore.

You do not want to do it.

You feel angry.

What chores do you do at home?

Maybe you did not get picked

for the team.

You feel like it is not fair.

Everyone feels angry at times.

You may want to yell when

you feel angry.

You may want to hit or kick.

**Why is it not
okay to hit
or kick?**

Maybe your brother

made you angry.

You may want to call

him a name.

Listen to your body when

you feel angry.

Try taking deep breaths.

This will help you calm down.

**What else
can you do to
calm down?**

Tell yourself it is going to be okay.

You may need time alone.

Find a friend or a parent.

Talk to them about how you feel.

This can help you feel better.

Picture Quiz

Which child is angry? Point to that picture.

Picture Glossary

accident
something that happens as a mistake

calm
not angry or upset

chores
jobs that have to be done every day

feeling
an emotion or thought

Read More

Butterfield, Moira. *Everybody Feels…Angry!* London: Quarto Publishing, 2016.

Graves, Sue. *Not Fair, Won't Share*. Minneapolis: Free Spirit Publishing, 2011.

Kawa, Katie. *I Feel Mad*. New York: Gareth Stevens, 2013.

Index

Photo Credits